sad boys are not my kink

Galia Admoni

DUNLIN PRESS

sad boys are not my kink
Galia Admoni
Published by Dunlin Press in 2025

Dunlin Press
Wivenhoe, Essex
dunlinpress.com | @dunlinpress

The right of Galia Admoni to be identified as the author of this work has been asserted in accordance with Section 77 of the Copyright, Designs and Patents Act 1988.

This book is sold subject to the condition that it shall not, by way of trade of otherwise, be lent, resold, hired out or otherwise circulated without the publisher's prior consent in any form of binding or cover other than which it is published and without a similar condition including this condition being imposed on the subsequent purchaser. No part of this publication may be reproduced, stored in or introduced into a retrieval system, or transmitted, in any form, or by any means (electronic, mechanical, photocopying, recording or otherwise) without the prior written permission of the publisher. Any person who does any unauthorised act in relation to this publication may be liable to criminal prosecution and civil claims for damages.

A CIP record of this book is available from the British Library.

ISBN: 978-1-7394038-8-1

Set in Adobe Garamond, Avant Garde Gothic Pro and Baskerville.
Book design by Ella Johnston.

Galia Admoni is the author of *Immediately after and then later* (Black Cat Press, 2024) and co-author of *Art Sundays* and *I get lost everywhere, you know this now* (Salo Press, 2025 / 2024). She has poems in *Prototype 6*, *The Rialto*, *Bad Lilies*, *The North* and others. She was commended in 2023 Primers and placed third in Briefly Write poetry prize 2022. She is also the Head of English at Friern Barnet School.

unravelling (v): undoing, investigating, solving or explaining something complicated or puzzling.	11

I have never met Joseph Gilgun

It's not like Google Maps announcing *you have arrived at your destination; you have arrived*	33
Day Trip	34
Night-time Fable	35
Barnaby	36
'Fucking Barnaby?!'	37
Joe's not that happy when I obsess over Paul McCartney	39
Joe dreams	40
Marmalade, Aisle 13	41
A recurring dream in which I am invited to join the star-studded sofa from the audience of a popular chat show that Joe has never actually been on	42
Room	43
Moon is a thief's song	44
Short Talk on Teeth *after Anne Carson*	45
In at least five episodes Joe seems like a proud dad	46
In the days where we don't go out I get erased a little at a time	47
I don't want to talk about Joe anymore	48
I don't want to think about Joe anymore	49
I don't want to hear Joe anymore	50
The night I almost but didn't actually meet Joe	51
At night	52
An unwelcome morning wthout him	53
After watching the YouTube video three times in a row I realise I might not be done writing about Joe after all	54
Thursday	55

Breadcrumbs

The algorithm on Instagram keeps showing me videos of Irish castles as if a fairytale is just at my fingertips	60
Would you like me to celebrate you in any way in particular?	61
Before (breadcrumbs)	62
Thursday	63
Friday	64
Saturday	65
Sunday	66
Monday (me)	67
Monday (you)	68
Tuesday morning	69
After (breadcrumbs)	70

Wendy

Origin of Space(s)	78
On Sunday 2nd April at the Magdalena Abakanowicz exhibition, I ask Wendy *'if we surveyed a hundred people, how many do you think would say it looks like a vulva?'*	80
On Saturday 22nd April after the Marguerite Humeau exhibition at White Cube Bermondsey, we both write about cunts in the coffee shop	81
On Sunday 30th April at the Tate Modern, Wendy and I look at sculptures, paintings, art films and photographs, and Wendy obsesses over the content guidance sign outside	82
On Sunday 30th April Wendy and I also go to see the Klint / Mondrian exhibition while I am accidentally dressed like a Mondrian painting	83
In the gallery Wendy gets upset when I point out a 500-year-old violin which has never been played	84
Evening Class	85
Pierced Hemisphere II *for Barbara (for Wendy)*	86
To Celebrate: A Sestina *after Wendy Allen*	87
Wendy and I both feel ugly at the beauty exhibition	89

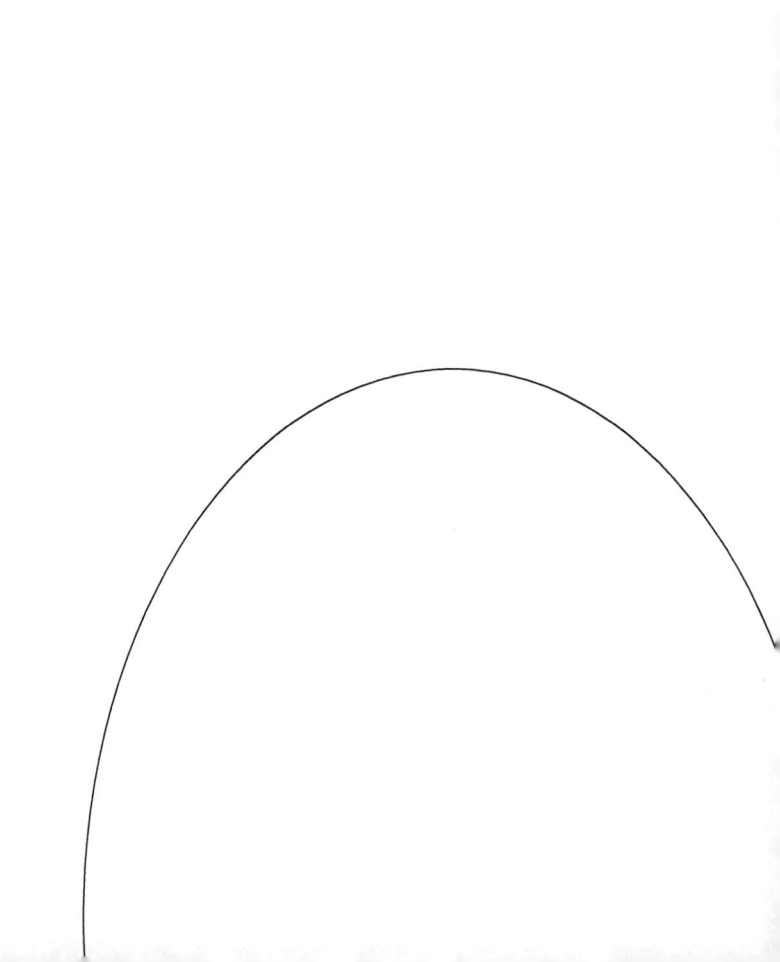

The boys I loved when I was young were moons

glowing velveteen spherical and decaying up close. Each month another emerged from behind a curtain. Out of an oyster shell. I dove for pearls beneath their depths. I astronauted myself. Undressed of gravity, I floated away.

unravelling (v): undoing, investigating, solving or explaining something complicated or puzzling.

1.

You stand in front of the mirror at home, adjusting your shirt. It's an old one, one you've had since before you met him. The shirt, the situation - it feels like one long unravelling. October, and the sudden remembering pulls on your victories like threads unravelling what you thought was strong. The mirror shows you angles you hadn't seen before, and now, you can't unsee them. You obsessively reread your diary from the him times, pages where you thought you could find clarity. You have only recently re-found the diary because of the news, and since then, you read it over and over, you scan it into your phone page by page so you can access it at any time. Then, December, and a friend mentions you as a person of interest to a documentary film maker, who calls you several times and wants to reassure you that what they're making is not just going to be a film about him, like the last, but also about the wider culture of the time. The news, the conversations, they all make the diary heavier, but you can't let it go. Written word and weight exist as proof of the conceptual idea of him. Suffix. Sometimes, you're secretly pleased he's not real to you anymore, except he is.

Do you continue to pull at the threads, or do you leave it alone?

Pull at the threads. Turn to page 14
Leave it alone. Turn to 7

2.

Then Friday, and a boy opposite you in the library picks up a book and whispers to it, *why are you being so secretive? let me read you* and it makes you want to cry. You cry. You don't ever stop crying.

Weeks pass. You obsessively research youth hostels, fancy hotels, places to escape, then immediately close all the browser windows and wash your hair furiously instead. You buy an expensive hairband you'll never wear.

Months pass. C starts sending you updates whenever *he* is in the news, and you wonder if you have seemed more alright than you should have. You respond exclusively in emojis whenever this happens and then spend hours wondering whether you picked the right one.

You keep trying to edit yourself, like a poem. It won't work.
Turn to 16

3.
anechoic (adj.): free from echo, a place where sound is deadened.

You sit, trembling, fingers clinging to the bed beneath you. You should get up, you should go, but for now, it's enough to stay here, paused in the quiet of your own wreckage.

You tell yourself that destruction implies meaning or the existence of something.

He forms a gun with his fingers, points to your head, pulls a face and says he couldn't really do it. You know he could.

You wonder how much longer you can keep trying to keep the parts of yourself together that want to break.

Let him. Turn to 6
Just let him. Turn to 11

4.
seafoam (n): created by agitation of dissolved organic matter and churned up by waves and wind.

You stand in a living room, the walls filled with pictures that ask you to feel something, to create meaning where none exists. You've always believed that art should be without the burden of meaning but he is looking at you for acknowledgement of his intelligence. You nod and say nothing. He says it feels like home. You think it feels like entering a film set where the cameras are already rolling. You nod and say nothing.

[Something too graphic is redacted here, and an incident report is misfiled in your memory]

The flat is always filled with expectation.
If you go again, you'll regret it.

Go again and again. Turn to 5
Maybe just once? Turn to 15

5.

On the way to him this time, you see the boy next to you on the tube text someone *we're going to have such a lovely time* and it makes you cry. You don't ever stop crying.

Once there, you wonder how many others have crossed this threshold, carrying the same unspoken weight.

Stay. Turn to 3
Go. Turn to 12

6.

You let him. Of course you do.

You wonder how many others have stood here, staring at the same ruin, trying to make sense of their own broken stories.

You didn't know the right way to say it, so –

No choices left. Turn to 16

7.

You turn from the diary
looking instead at the mushrooming sky.
Words no longer matter.
You try to close your eyes, but they only
seem to open wider. This isn't a thing you can
erase with a blink.
It's there,
lingering like echo.

Sinkhole. Turn to 13
Green for go. Turn to 8

8.

Your path is littered with half-formed thoughts. You whisper to yourself, *That one. No, not that one, maybe that one.* You're searching for something – what, exactly, you're not sure.

Don't look now, but that's the one. Exactly that.

That one. Turn to 5
No, that one. Turn to 15

9.

[redacted]

Go back. Turn to 5.
Go further back. Turn to 15.

10.

Shift into a lulling / touch starved
You can almost hear the sound of things falling apart

Turn to 16

11.

You let him. Of course you do.

Definitely, definitely try not to upset him.

You wonder how many others have stood here, staring at the same ruin, trying to make sense of their own broken stories.

You didn't know what question to ask, so –

No choices left. Turn to 16

12.

You are drawn to the ones that can't look you in the eye and there are plenty to choose from, if you're not picky. You have a talent for performing your happiness.

You want to forget him, so you see him everywhere.

Pretend you haven't made a mistake. Turn to 2
Try to fix your mistake. Turn to 10

13.

Your body becomes a sinkhole opening up under all the beds in history.

You don't understand it but you know what it means.

His mouth is brine and so salt becomes sickening.
You notice that the bed fabric is spoiled from use,
but you have a talent for performing mechanised desire,
so he only sees longing in the loathing.

And all along the bedroom ceiling
there stretches a line of fire.

Go back. Turn to 5
Go further back. Turn to 15

14.

It sits in on your bedside table like a threat.
The paper crackles like argument,
like something you were never supposed to say.
"Do you regret it?" it asks, but you
already know the answer.
The words won't fix anything.
This is not a thing that can be
methodically deconstructed.
But words make a place
for the truth to sink in,
at least.

They are –

seafoam. Turn to 4
[redacted]. Turn to 9

15.

The man is a wolf who is a man who is actually a wolf.
You listen for hunger in his moans.
You make everything worse this way.

His kiss tastes apathy.

Stay. Turn to 3
Leave. Turn to 12

16.
lacuna (n) – an unfilled space.

You start at the point of loss. The choices you made have led you here, but there's only one way forward now. You wish you could map the places where you like to be touched but you don't remember anymore. You wonder why no one has ever thought to ordinance survey your body. Crosshatch shade into valleys or rivulets of skin. You wish you had set aside a compass but there are no coordinates to write out. Memories concatenate. You think – *Why make something to destroy it?* You take a long hard look in the mirror. You see the whole mechanism but not its component parts.

You wonder how many others have stood here, staring at the same ruin, trying to make sense of their own broken stories.

One last choice in the quiet of night, but not your own.

Questionnaire for post-incident elimination policy information

If the case is a landmark then does that make it:
    a) beautiful?
    b) immovable?
    c) something to add to the list of top tourist attractions in town?

When they say *what's done cannot be undone* and speak of Shakespeare as if it were real are you:
    a) impressed?
    b) sickened?
    c) a bit of both, but you'll never tell?

You're waiting for the next line. What is it again?
    a) *To bed*
    b) *To bed*
    c) *To bed*

When there is no gate left to knock on, does it even make a sound?
    a) …
    b) …
    c) *Ha!*

And what noise does the night make for you these days?
    a) The moon groans into the sky like a bloated corpse.
    b) The dark is a dull repetitive thump. *Please make it stop.*
    c) When I hear the neighbour's TV, I throw a party.

And where, if anywhere, do you think you'll feel OK to be touched again?
    a) My hair, when it's stroked like Grecian stone.
    b) It is biblical.
    c) It speaks with whispers that sound like gunfire.

bed-dream

    to imagine
        the sounds you make in the dark

    without bedding down in the jamminess of you
      falling into shameless hours

    feeling your borders
        lithe   possessed   plum

    merging ornately
        pressing all parts   to finish

        a peak   wrecked   to oblivion
    entirely there   and also lost –

    an impossibility

     what resonance
        or quality   you must create

I have never met Joseph Gilgun

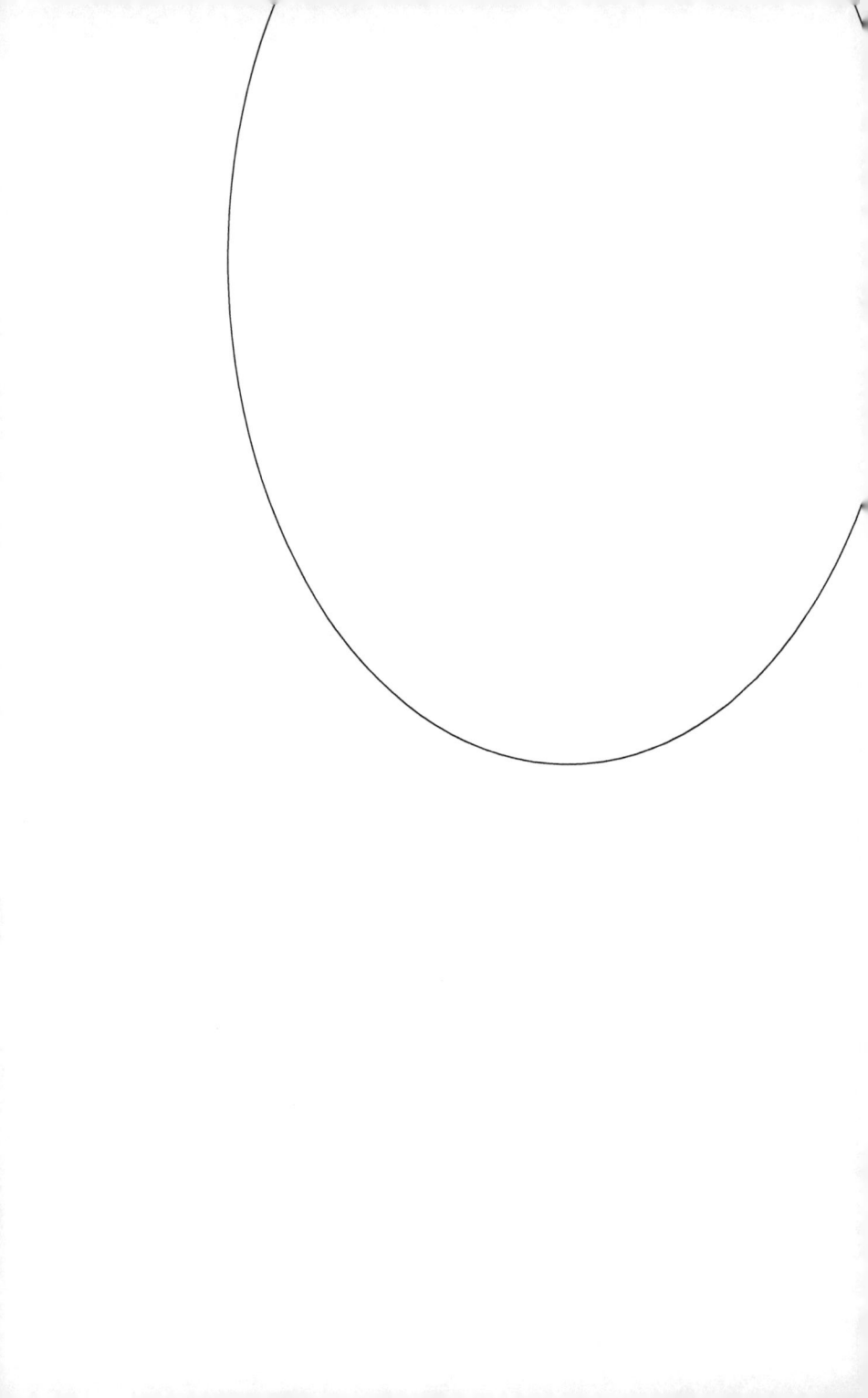

It's not like Google Maps announcing *you have arrived at your destination;* you have arrived

If people asked me why *(if they knew, they would)* then I would say it's because no one talks of people like us because we're not important. We're just the ones standing alone at someone else's wedding *(again)*. Lying awake at night wondering whether to do it now, and alone, so that our mums have a chance to be grandmas before they die. Yes. I would say *why not live with someone you choose?* And *why not choose for that someone to be an imaginary friend who has the face and voice of Joseph Gilgun?* Or a pink elephant who speaks exclusively in metaphors? Or even a God?

Sometimes, there are days where you've just done this --massive thing-- and there's no one to talk to. And so, day by day, you let another piece in because you're not whole in yourself. And so, when a *'Joe'* arrives it might be an extra mug of tea *here* and a duvet pushed against your bare legs at night *there* until one evening you find yourself on the sofa shouting *'Fringe!'* Out loud. Laughing. Pointing at the TV because an actress is sporting a fringe when she didn't have one before and you're not actually talking to no one or even just yourself after all. And it's all pink elephants and Gods from here on out.

If people asked me what use a pink elephant is, alone, in a lockdown *(if they were feeling particularly sassy, they might)* then I'd say, maybe, pink elephants are no use. And I'd glare back. And if people asked me what use a God is when your neighbour suddenly dies before he's 40; his body and whole life lying just through the wall you share, left to be catalogued by infantile police folk who complain loudly about their bosses at 3am outside your front door, eating McDonald's on the stairs dressed in blue plastic overalls when you come home from work for five days in a row, as if it's totally normal that someone is dead, like --actually dead-- right there *(if they were feeling particularly nasty, they might)* then I'm not sure what I'd say. I'd say, maybe, *you should probably choose yourself a new companion. Perhaps listen out for a Tardis landing in your garden. Or listen out for someone who might already have been there all along*.*

*when I first typed this word it autocorrected to 'alone' – *just saying…*

Day Trip

In half term Joe and I walk along the Southbank and it's much the same as always. The city is all greyscale water, giant sky and flash of red or blue of boat; a palimpsest of new*old* bricks. There's a pigeon, of course, gnarl-footed. It nods as it passes. A plastic bag whispers through the water in agreement. I say I want some coffee; maybe some cake. Something sweet. Joe gets out his vape and says nothing. I try to make him love the city as much as I do, though country boys can never stand the grey. At the water's edge we stop; hold hands. He is there; stoic, heavy. It's weight that makes things real, so I know he's there by the ache in my arm. He weighs me down. When I get back to the flat, even the kettle smokes like him.

Night-time Fable

Can you kiss with those things in and by kiss I mean other things? You see, there's something about metal on flesh. Your gold teeth are cold on me. You take a bite of thigh, the fire spreads and before too long I cannot help but turn my insides out for you. Notice where you place your hands when you go down on me. Towards the end of the week you become more vivid and fuck me in the way I think you actually would. It's all about you. Our bedroom altercations ring out under the pompom trimmed pendant shade. You're there in the mirrored door of the wardrobe because I don't want to see the truth.

Barnaby

"…and I think it's
an IPA, or maybe
a Pilsner..."
he said, and
it was evident from
the trailing off of
his voice that
we were having
one of
the most
boring
conversations
at
the
party.

'*Fucking Barnaby?!*'

Yes, we meet on an app but it turns out we have a mutual friend (a man who I once kisssed at a pedestrian crossing at midnight and who's now married to a skinny blonde) and our first date is OK. He suggests a niche Hampstead pub and arrives twenty minutes late.

Joe's already angry because he hates when people are late.

He talks about his mother. He talks about his podcast. Within a few more minutes it's clear that he's got the stripy t-shirt of an overgrown indie boy whose hair is at least 30% of his personality.

I wonder if people think the same about me
Joe scoffs – hair is a sensitive topic.

We don't hug at the train station at the end. But, through a series of texts over the following days, we decide to meet for a second date.

'Are you mad?' says Joe / I say 'Mad's not what I'd call it'.

So I suggest a pub five minutes' walk from my house and arrive on time. I wear black, as usual, but it's textures on textures to try and get tactile. He asks to try on my coat-

'*Mate, he thinks he's Mick Jagger!*'

    and it's not long before the velvet of my dungarees works

thank god / 'pah!'

    and he's stroking my thigh. Not long before we're walking around the corner to my flat. Not long before suddenly we're topping and tailing on the sofa like a tween-sleepover watching reruns of a generic comedy panel show

wait, what's happening?

      and he's massaging my socked foot like we're elderly. He's talking about how he needs to leave soon in a low, apologetic voice, and of course it's then that Joe appears in the doorway.

slow clapping / gold grin on show

'That you have to persuade the man to stay says it all', croons Joe.

That, through the derision in the voice I can hear in my head about *what dickheads we both are* in this moment isn't lost on me. But there's a man in my house and I'm not sorry, *'even if his name is Barnaby'.*

So I don't waste a moment. It's the weight of him that makes me persist. Joe goes quiet and I don't even mind that I'm not really there.

'Seriously Joe, stop it' / derision from the corner / is it jealousy?

There's nothing of note about the rest of the evening. So when I'm at work the next day, and the receptionists giggle, say they 'caught me' kissing a man at the station in the morning, I don't think about the fact that what they actually caught was an exercise in attempting to control my imagination and live, for at least one evening, in the real world whatever the hell that is. In fact, I don't really feel caught at all, because they don't know who's really waiting for me at home.

slow clapping / gold grin on show

Joe's not that happy when I obsess over Paul McCartney

because however hard he tries, he'll
always be fragile, though

seeing *his* name in
these poems

(instead of Paul McCartney's)

will help. I imagine him reading
about himself.

Joe dreams

    about his Grandma Sadie, the smell of

        stale Superkings, strong tea and the

            machete in her drawer that could

                chop a child's head off.

He dreams about his dad. *He was a*

        fucking hero, metal working his way

            through the factory in his mind.

A classic man of place.

        Working with hard things

            never hardened him.

Marmalade, Aisle 13

For me, it's the jams.
One glimpse of an orange jar
and I'm back in my grandma's kitchen.
Metal stairs by the back door where she
kept her houseplants.

Coral pink bathroom, Shake and Vac
on the carpeted stairs, mint creams
and Casualty, checking her
lottery numbers.
Every Saturday night was

an occasion. We'd play shops
with her shoes. She made bolognaise
with lamb, toast with marmalade
instead of jam. Pickled beetroot,
pinking scrambled eggs for Sunday breakfast.

This is a different *species* of grief.

A recurring dream in which I am invited to join the star-studded sofa from the audience of a popular chat show that Joe has never actually been on

From his velvet swiveller, Graham smiles and gestures for me to join him, in the middle of the show.

Some nights he even runs into the crowd to take my hand and guide me down the steps, to the stage.

I sit on the sofa with the stars, different most nights, though Joe is always there.

Room

All afternoon / dry air and memory of rain

In the bedroom the space is bursting with you

It is summer but you are not here

I will fill myself with you

What you are not / I will be

Moon is a thief's song

A crook of moon / cracked the crescent /

pocketed the swell / whistled over the glow /

A low hum of crime

I keep indoors / tromboning the curtains /

stealthing a peek

There are no real consequences / living only at night /

only / you have to sing a little quieter

Short Talk on Teeth
after Anne Carson

Fed up to the back of them / sometimes

teeth that preach of care and pride are gleaming white / but we

make ours gold / Not long in them / No skin off them / Refuse

to take a golden shovel to them / instead just bare them / To

lie through them / descend into cavities / make them itch / We'll take

some of yours for ours *(they are removable after all)* / and care

about as much as wisdom allows / Still we say / of

all the ways to crumble and crunch and crush ourselves /

be warned / Base metals hint to baser instincts / In

superficial displays ours glisten and gleam / but only in protest

In at least five episodes Joe seems like a proud dad

so I take the folic acid / inject the hormones / make my body a facility / I am battery / teeming / I do not rend / I keep it all on ice /

In one, he holds a rabbit like a baby
so I learn to crochet / keep lists of names / smile at tiny socks /

He has time or no desire or too much choice
so I say / I will do this on my own (if I have to) / I am still young / *smile with teeth* / I have made myself / ready / (wound up Jack-in-the-box) / ready / and just as tense

In the days where we don't go out I get erased a little at a time
    scrubbed, then laid over with boracic lint-
    sterilised with antiseptic.

I just need a little help, somewhere to rest,
    but all the chairs are filled with his feelings –
    so we average out our misery.

And sometimes I'll fight and he won't,
    and it's a pyrrhic victory if there is one at all, with a
    forehead that's just a mishmash of sovereign marks.

Him, sitting in my seat just because he can.
    making me feel bird-like for a while; tiny.
    But then it's small, *small*, and not in a good way.

I don't want to talk about Joe anymore

but I ask whether they watched *Brassic* last night.
I say *acting is tough* but really I mean
I want to make things easier for him.

It's less complicated with Charlotte,
who knows, though I still want to
apologise each time I
accidentally mention
his name.

I don't want to think about Joe anymore

but he pushes in regardless,
bullishly indifferent.

He asks me what it means to not exist.
I tell him I'll think about it.
He shouts at me to answer.
I want my tongue to come loose.

Because how can I tell him he's only the
belch of something real? And how could I explain
to the others that he's real to me?

There's no balm for
this type of breakdown.

I don't want to hear Joe anymore

but it's hard to see any kind of future if you
can't even make it to the drawer
to get some pants to put on –
most of your efforts spent on trying to
keep the houseplants alive.

From the next room Joe shouts
something sweary and insulting about
the dog or the shopping.

He's so natural – it's like we've somehow
done this before, except we haven't,
because none of it's real.

I used to think that when you tugged on a
thread like that the whole world would
unravel, but somehow I can know it's all
brainwaves and still hear the click of his
vape in the next room.
Smoke and mirrors, eh?

The night I almost but didn't actually meet Joe

The room was fluorescent
and the plastic chairs were too close together
and I'd had one beer too many *(one)*
and it was a school night
and I probably wasn't northern enough
and Charlotte wasn't keen on the embarrassment
and there were too many people in the crowd
and I should've lost more weight first anyway
and he probably had a girl at home
and I watched him open the door
and the evening was over
and he'd left the room
and then I was sitting alone
and so I've still never actually met him

At night

he smiles (or I smile for him) in
shadows of the flat –
living his invisible-man life. The only
real*pretend* friend
I've had.

A womb-warm throb weighing-in
heavy. A moth against a
well-lit window. A flash in
the corner of an eye.

His low-slow night-voice
lullabying. His mind
(but really mine) -
susurrations.

I'm so content I feel
sick. Reaching out
for his body,
which has never been there.

An unwelcome morning without him

Take me back to where we left things /
I want to feel like grass, or as alive, or even

just as green / how things could seem (or even be) if
you were here. You, taking root in

my wetness, or dew in mornings of blue / half
asleep (or more) but full of joy. The passing of

mornings like these goes by
unnoticed / except for the light.

After watching the YouTube video three times in a row I realise I might not be done writing about Joe after all

wake up   have a love with him   make a brew
take me meds   take him for a walk   painting
    feverish

    ruined all me clothes
    fucked up me flat

There's never a plan   *with colours / the approach*
That's a good example   You can see how
fast that's gone out
That's terrible   Lost me temper with that
That's one I   shoulda gone back to

I THINK THERE'S SOMETHING CHANGING HERE
(I DON'T THINK IT'LL   EVER END)

there's a lot of that   crowds of faces
on top of each other   to the point where
from a distance
                     zoom in   missing elements
ears   eyes   of being unfinished
unreachable

                            wouldn't want watching you

Thursday

Read an article about actors in British *Vogue*[1]

Watched a film of *Pride and Prejudice*[2]

Read a Wendy Cope poem about her lover[3]

---

[1] *Why is no one putting Joe in British vogue?*

[2] *Why is no one putting Joe in a period drama?*

[3] *Why is no one putting Joe in a p-*

At midnight on New Year's Eve Charlotte and I each eat twelve grapes while sitting under the dining table

i.
        because I'm jealous of my friends' unhappy marriages

ii.
I dread another year without
        the first thrill of knowing what a heart is
                      capable of
        the ache of sleepless
            4am next to someone
                wondering
                    who loves more or will
                        love longest

iii.
I can't conceive of that 4am any more than I can
            remember
            what it feels like to be
                      kissed
            or dry up dishes
                someone else has washed

iv.
I am resolute
        in not wishing out loud / keeping the spell intact

v.
Grapes are silent hopes
No more
        my life doesn't look like I thought it would by now

vi.
One grape is rotten   I eat it anyway

vii.
By five past twelve
we've shuffled
wordlessly
to our beds
for shame
because
we
should
be
more
than
this

viii.
I think all the hours between 12 and 4am
I think *I think too much*

ix.

. . .

x.
Eventually my dreams are vines but where the grapes should be are shrivelled hearts, which is better than the grapes, for dramatic purposes. There's a swivel chair dizziness to the dream world and my dream self thinks amusedly about the way that movement is strangely tangible in the dream world because although I've never been on a rollercoaster I've seen enough of them to know how one might feel.

xi.
At the other end of the dream someone distant and impatient repeats a refrain of

> *strip the leaves off the vines for me*
> *for me*
> *for me!*

xii.
I wake with the smell of rotting fruit in my nostrils

Breadcrumbs

The algorithm on Instagram keeps showing me videos of Irish castles as if a fairytale is just at my fingertips

I keep thinking about a boy I might like, who lives over 300 miles away – *damn that giant body of water just between us there.* We don't know each other at all. Have never met. Two entirely separate stories with a single page each in a shared book.

When I tell him I'm 34 over text one night, he, spicy and hungover, asks if I have any hang-ups about kissing 28 year olds, as if he's asking about kissing frogs. I say I suppose it depends on the 28 year old and in his next reply he uses my name. It is golden. Crystalline. He wouldn't even have to find a lamp to summon this genie.

Crush is a terrible and perfect word for what this is. It implies weight; burden. He is dove feather / poison apple. But I have been mid-story *Cinderella'd* so many times now that I would not be surprised if the shoe fits someone else. Or shatters altogether after midnight.

Would you like me to celebrate you in any way in particular?

I tell him I want to be in his poems
I want him cuntstruck
and this is a problem that solves itself –

I am ambrosial

He has never written about getting head
Never had head good enough to write about
and this is a problem I can solve-

challenge accepted

In only eight weeks we have come
to the edge of something.
I have an ache for that life and
this life to be
the only life –

singular

and this is a problem I cannot solve.

Before (breadcrumbs)

I
Will be
waiting for   sounds like
           love
Sounds

                                    exactly what
I needed (heart) (heart)
        kissing
                              no regrets
                                    Of course
                        the best
    Would

                        live up to it

  flirting   (hearts) (hearts) Delighted (tongue out) I'm a big fan of it   kiss?   everything
        caving to romance

    Still wanna
                    The sweetest (heart)

                                            Still wanna
            Appreciate you   always (heart)
                              Appreciate you   still up for
  something   it's all we have   I just couldn't   And I am now   (smile)

Thursday

I buy bread and good coffee in the morning, for imagined breakfasts, because my mother has raised me to be a good host, especially to men.

I spend the afternoon panic cleaning. Three months has been a long time. This afternoon feels longer.

I go to my poetry class in the evening. I'm excited. Something important is happening for the first time in a long time.

I wait for you to arrive (late) at the meeting place in Tottenham Court Road.

I take us to Soho Theatre Bar for a drink. I am wearing the red dress and gold watch ring that Wendy has said make me beautiful.

I take us home and tell you to have my bed. I'll sleep in the spare room. We've only met for the first time tonight. We don't have to rush. You kiss me goodnight like a promise.

Friday

The bread on the counter stays untouched this morning, like me, while I wait for you to finish the work you said you had to do. Instead, we breakfast at the local café and are awkward over avocado toast.

By the evening we're eating falafel and chatting about how this isn't going to go anywhere.

We play the game of 'who is a couple' while obviously not being a couple.

You kiss me goodnight again for absolutely no reason.

Saturday

Last night I pretended there was something wrong with my mum on the way home so I could go to her flat and have a panic attack without you next to me and today I am feeling ok, which is either because of the Propranolol or because everything is always much worse at nighttime and now it's daytime, see, it's lovely weather out and we're both dressed and ready and we decide not to eat any breakfast because let's just go out and enjoy the sunshine while we can, wave farewell to the bread on the counter, no need for you today, mister loaf! I have bought us tickets to see Joe Dunthorne speak in Newington Green Meeting House which I thank past me for doing because it's one more hour where I won't have to make happy conversation while trying to ignore the thoughts going round in my head about how awful I must be because you've taken one look at me and decided that three months of speaking every day is meaningless compared to how ugly you must find me and why did you get on a plane to come here if you were just going to tell me you're moving to Barcelona and don't want to start anything serious and also why are you using the word 'start', which is really quite hurtful actually, when three months of talking feels not like starting but being quite a lot of the way in the middle of something actually and now I feel guilty about thinking bad things about you when I'm probably just overreacting because I've been rejected and as you can see I'm definitely not having a panic attack any more I'm fine I'm fine I'm fine I'm fine I'm f-

Sunday

In the gallery I don't feel moved by anything and say out loud that I haven't found the one yet. I'm talking about the paintings, of course, but I'm looking at the back of your head while I say it. I'm pointing and gesturing wildly right at you but you don't seem to notice.

In the gallery Wendy says in hushed tones so you can't hear that fighting the urge to cry for three days has made me beautiful.

In the gallery I look at sculptures and paintings of bodies and realise I don't have one of my own. My body is made by others' hands. You won't touch me, so I don't exist.

Monday (me)

Just one hour after you get on a train to the airport to go back home, your books are re-shelved, the notes you wrote me held between their pages. I won't look at them again. Within twelve hours the towels and sheets you used have been washed. You have left an empty water glass behind the bedroom door which takes me fifteen hours to find. By the time you have gone the bread I bought on Thursday has gone mouldy from the inside. I throw it out. And though I can't quite bring myself to delete the photos of you from my phone, it only takes a day for you to be entirely wrung out from my flat, at least.

Monday (you)

I imagine you giving us an aerial burial on the flight home.

Tuesday morning

there's a card on my work desk from Kathy.
It says, simply, *I'm sorry he wasn't the one.*

After (breadcrumbs)

I remember that I don't know how to act around bread which is why I don't keep it in my house.

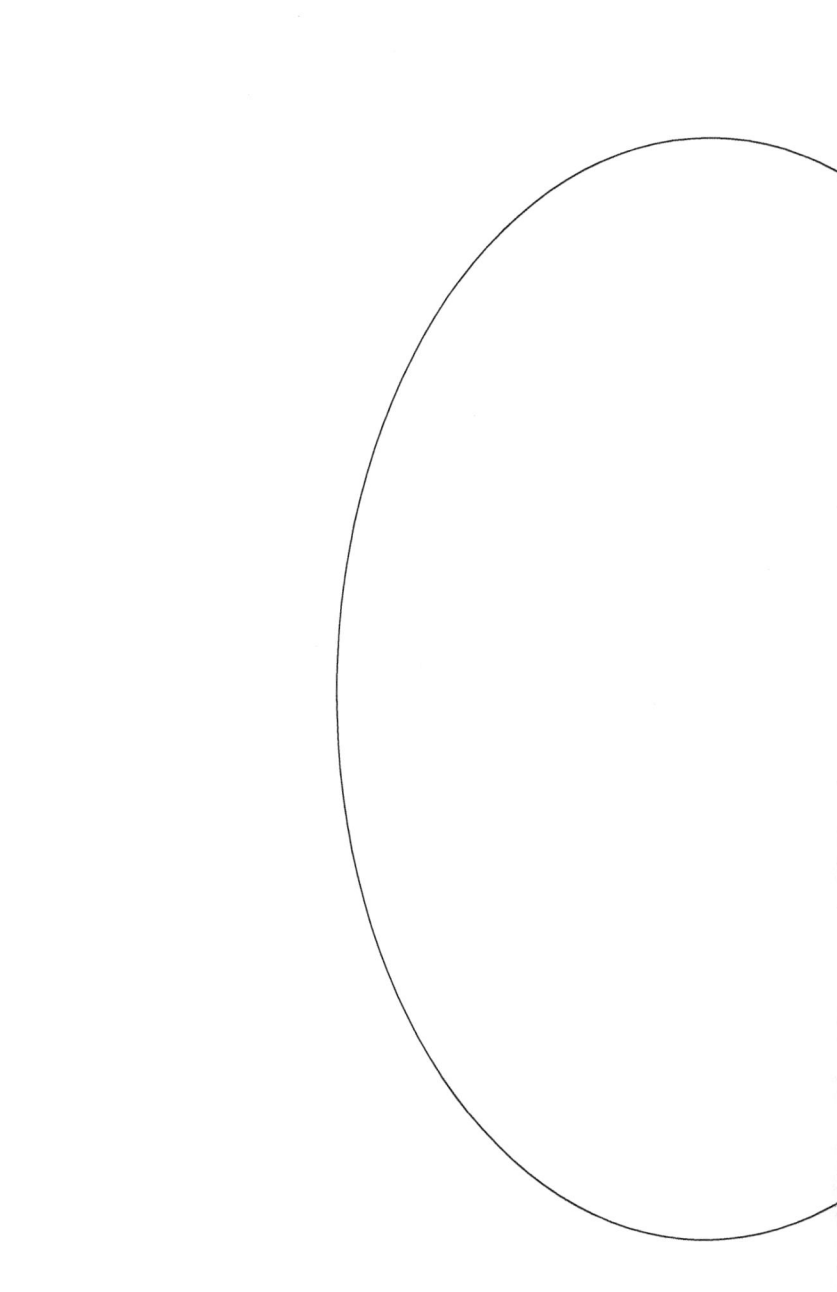

Further evidence that you are a true agent of chaos

Once when I was eight I invited ten friends to see the view from the top of a building for my birthday party. Only seven came but that was ok, seven was enough for a celebration. When they all arrived though, it was clear they didn't actually want to be there. As we started to climb, each step was a ringing out of *Why didn't she want to go dry ski slope skiing?* or *I can't believe my mum made me come to this!* but I didn't care. I wanted to scale this building. I had to. There was something about the way it rose above it all that appealed to me. Was it aspirational? I didn't know much back then, but I somehow knew I would feel better when I was at the top. It turned out to be a cloudy day though, even in June, and the only way any of us could see the view from our short eight-year-old bodies was by taking turns to stand on each other's shoulders, peering through convenient breaks in the cloud bank when they presented themselves. This wasn't a great strategy because we were eight, and weak, and also no one really cared about the view except me. A few of my friends took pity on me after a while and tried to lift me up. Once or twice I was able to see a snapshot of green below. It looked velvet. I wanted more. We tried again and I saw tiny toy cars circling as if on tracks, like they had no choice. One last try allowed for an image of a haybale on fire. This, it turned out, was the last straw. I fell from my friend's shoulders, directly on to my hands and knees, and I cried. There was blood. I blinked through the tears and then it turned out it wasn't my eighth birthday after all, it was yesterday. And the building was your functional marriage to someone else and your published books and the friends were all my failed relationships and unfinished poems and high functioning anxiety and the cloud bank was the thing that meant we stopped talking properly and the tears were, well they were actually, to be fair, just tears.

Night List

i
a road is being paved by men in high vis jackets

ii
a girl is holding the hair of another girl / streaming vomit and tears fall into a gutter next to a traffic cone

iii
doorways like dovecotes but less inviting / curated plants like East London haircuts stand bullish like sentries on doorsteps / moss falls freely in waves by their sides / it does not care

iv
a couple kisses wet and loud on the tube (it is octopus squelch / muddy grass / dog shit under trainer)

v
night air is a cold compress to the forehead / it says be better / be better / at least be well

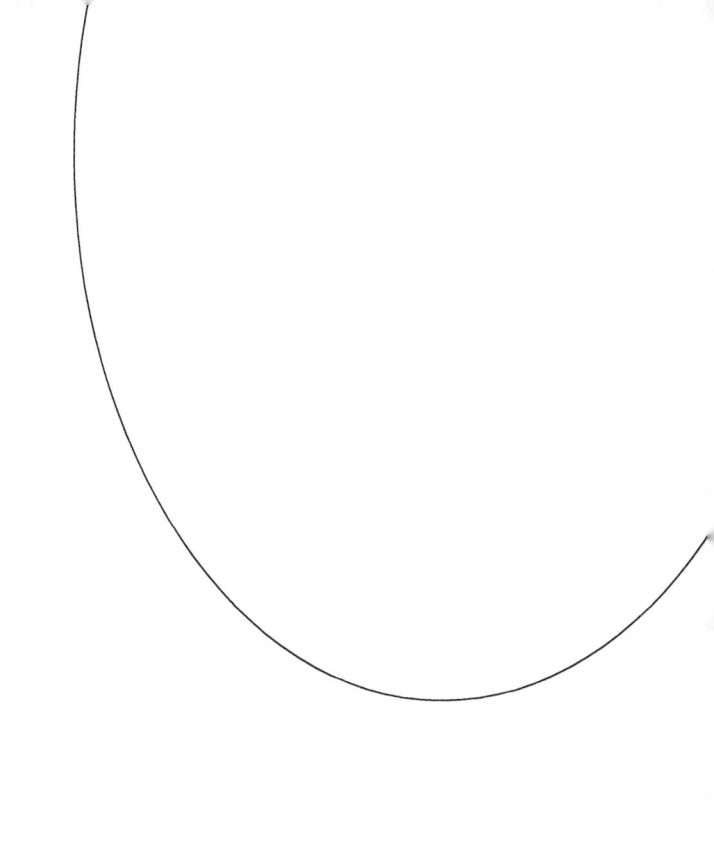

Wendy

Origin of Space(s)

Wendy and I look at paintings with gaps / holes / cracks but there's nothing missing / lacking. We can't explain the three heads of the *Allegory of Prudence* any more than we could explain the magic here that makes hours liminal / how walking through centuries of brushstrokes turns almost-strangers to friends in mere minutes. How Michaelangelo's Baptist, who 'gazes inward in possible awareness of the future' makes us uncomfortable / why the probable-possible space in *The Manchester Madonna* appeals to us.

While we walk, I quiz Wendy on the names of paintings I instinctively know she'll like / withholding their true titles until she's tried several times. *An orgasm of colour*, she says. I point out how unlikely a 16th century painting entitled 'orgasm' would be and immediately hate myself for it. Wendy's love of body seeps into everything / morphs Juno into an invitation / and I see her picturing this painting on the wall above the bed where she meets with her lover who she doesn't know I know about. I imagine her orgasm in the breast milk that spurts into the centre of the canvas / *The Origin of the Milky Way* is sort of like the orgasm of the universe.

Watching Kehinde Wiley's *The Prelude* gives us both a backache that neither of us mention at the time, but we're so irrationally connected to the strangers on screen we can't move away. Nature / changes / humans / change. Big screens with big ideas. But over coffee, Wendy asks me not about the white expanses of snow or the way in which the capital 'R' Romantic writing of Wordsworth's poem was recreated on screen, but about the performers' red make-up / *do I think she could pull it off?* It's an absurd question, I think to myself, because I can't imagine a single thing Wendy could say or do that I wouldn't think was perfection / I spend most of the day trying not scare her off with adoration. I also think that Wendy would paint her whole body period-red if she could / She'd swim in her mooncup.

In another room, later in the day, Renoir's brushstrokes mirror our conversation – feathery at first then reworked with harder contours. It's a new friendship / this. But I know it's going well when she likes Stubbs' horse as much as I do / when we see it leaping from the far wall as we round a corner / just like I remembered. She gets it like she gets me. Though it's obvious in its alone-ness, it's not *empty* of rider / background / equipment. It is / in fact / *free*.

On Sunday 2nd April at the Magdalena Abakanowicz exhibition, I ask Wendy *'If we surveyed a hundred people, how many do you think would say it looks like a vulva?'*

A rendering of the gallery visit is
    the underside of a woodlouse
A rendering of the gallery visit is
    the underside of a woodlouse / a closed shell
A rendering of the gallery visit is
the underside of a woodlouse / a closed shell / organic masses
A rendering of the gallery visit is
    the underside of a woodlouse / a closed shell / organic masses / throbbing / angry / devoid of activity
A rendering of the gallery visit is
    the underside of a woodlouse / a closed shell / organic masses / throbbing / angry / devoid of activity / mercenary
A rendering of the gallery visit is
    the underside of a woodlouse / a closed shell / organic masses / throbbing / angry / devoid of activity / mercenary / petrified in all senses of the word
A rendering of the gallery visit is
    the underside of a woodlouse / a closed shell / organic masses / throbbing / angry / devoid of activity / mercenary / petrified in all senses of the word / an *unease of formation*
A rendering of the gallery visit is
    the underside of a woodlouse / a closed shell / organic masses / throbbing / angry / devoid of activity / mercenary / petrified in all senses of the word / an *unease of formation* / imperceptibly unseen

On Saturday 22nd April after the Marguerite Humeau exhibition at White Cube Bermondsey, we both write about cunts in the coffee shop

Recounting the gallery sequentially is squares / tiles / erased forms from hives of skilled craftspeople.

Everything is body parts even without Wendy. Everything is the crocheted jumper unfinished on my sofa.

Honeycombs dovecote which implies emptiness / which implies the gaps from tiles / the unfinished jumper on my sofa.

She looks at mushrooms / their undersides baleen / line up / breathe / crease like open curtains.

I have no time for mushrooms.

Coral is porous / open / round like orgasm (of course) / but empty of wet affection.

I have more time for coral.

A displacement of landscapes / a vulva flowers in one corner as an invitation.

In a few days I will only remember the flavour / ambrosial / and a worshipping of all the empty.

On Sunday 30th April at the Tate Modern, Wendy and I look at sculptures, paintings, art films and photographs, and Wendy obsesses over the content guidance sign outside

A retelling of the day is a form of collage:

of things salvaged
of things charred
of things reconstructed and simplified
of objects emphasising an interconnectedness with forces larger than ourselves
of objects evoking the subversive power of artists' previous work
of pieces unifying disparate elements like fragments of furniture alongside florals, to create a new kind of harmony
of pieces reflecting disruptions between creation and destruction
of delicate paintwork pierced with violence, with holes that are deeply inviting – galvanic, like the potential for orgasm
of Wendy saying that the paintings we see are my poems in art forms
of the sign that declares that *This display shows photography and film where artists use their bodies in performances as a form of activism*
of the fact that this is a perfect rendering of Wendy's poems

On Sunday 30th April Wendy and I also go to see the Klint / Mondrian exhibition while I am accidentally dressed like a Mondrian painting

Wendy insists on taking a photo to memorialise the occasion

I don't need a photo

In the gallery Wendy gets upset when I point out a 500-year-old violin which has never been played

The gallery is a physical reconstruction of this poem before it's made.

Object I
an empty coffee cup with dregs from the coffee consumed before the gallery visit

Object IIa
a map of the gallery, some pieces circled in red pen

Object IIb
red pen used to circle pieces on the gallery map

Object III
yellow ring at the bottom of the bag replaced with vintage stone ring from the gallery shop

Object IV-VII
Selfies, photographed 2023, printed 2024, courtesy of the artist

Object VIII
laughter, bottled from the second coffee break of the day

Evening Class

You post about Anne Sexton on Instagram
while I discuss her in my poetry class.

I don't know the reference and feel
stupid. I think about finding her books in

the Poetry Library, where you and I have
visited, coveted and planned where our

own words might fit on the shelves. Yours will
be there soon – little birds nesting next to Sexton's.

You will wear yellow at the book launch,
of course, and read aloud to people - their

mouths forming O in wonder, O in
mimicry of the perfect orgasms you write about so

well. I think about looking at bookshelves with
you, while my tutor give us free time to write.

Try on a new voice she says. I only ever want to
try on yours.

Pierced Hemisphere II *for Barbara (for Wendy)*

You / handle my curved form / reinforce the outlines / asphaltic skin / configuration of shape / I am porous / open / for you / a mouth forming O / thinking of a sound that isn't surprise / opening a window / passing through / emptying out / like rounds of empty shells / falling from a fired gun / I tilt upwards / see inside / see shadow / bevelled / tapering / piercing smooth circularity

To Celebrate: A Sestina *after Wendy Allen*

The word *fuck* comes pre erased
when you are a woman who enjoys writing
about sex. Watch the way orgasm curls like guilt
in smoke circles and disappears from the poem.
When I describe the speaker's pleasure in orgasm
the dismissive silence that follows in response confirms this.

O reader, let my speaker be this
bold, vituperative woman who has erased
all thoughts of anything and everything but orgasm –
owns only words that lead to writing
poem on poem on poem
about sex, without guilt.

O reader, in your dismissive silence, watch the way guilt
disappears like smoke circles from this
poem.
Watch how this poem confirms that pleasure will never be erased –
how I describe the speaker dismissing pre erased writing
and responding in printed orgasm.

O reader, here is your orgasm
No guilt!
Golden gilt circles   O   *fuck*   writing
    this
  erased
      poem!

O reader, see now how this poem
fades like an orgasm.
Enjoy the way silent words are curled and erased
when I describe the speaker beginning to feel guilt
at the quality of this
writing.

Fuck this writing
Fuck this poem
Fuck this
Fuck to orgasm
Fuck without guilt
Fuck to be erased

Writing an orgasm
into this poem without guilt
means this pleasure can never be erased

Wendy and I both feel ugly at the beauty exhibition

i.

We take a photo in the pink room
It's all *Husbands bringing their ugly wives to a windmill, to be transformed into beautiful women*
and Helena Rubenstein examines her schedule for an average day in New York
We work
The photo doesn't

ii.

We take a photo in the blue room
We both have spots though mine is bigger
You start to realise what's real to me when we see the piece that says
You're fat
and gross
your arms
make me
want to
puke

iii.

    I take a photo of Wendy in the Beauty Sensorium without her knowing
        We try to get at the goo but it's trapped behind glass
        We can't disinter a first-hand sensory experience here
    We talk about reconstruction in the space filled with reconstructed
                cosmetic recipes
        We talk about our understanding of how to exploit the tactile
                properties of natural materials

iv.

We take selfies in all of the reflective surfaces
                                    which is the opposite of their
purpose but we are shameless

v.

We do not take a photo in the black room with (almost) all of [the artist's] dead mother's things

There is a tender intimacy in the   silence   of the room
which
    crystalises   when we realise   what we're looking at

There is a tension   between the beauty of it

    and its
        weight

Pinned to the bedframe a note says *'inside the dimly lit room standing small still and quiet under the high rounded ceiling I am waiting'* while inside this dimly lit room we stand small still and quiet under the high rounded ceiling and wait.

In one moment we know *this* has transcended into something   more
We will never disentangle ourselves from   *this*

Fragile   like a whispered song or   symphony of things
                      unspoken

Your tear is on my hand then
                is suddenly
                a universe
                an expanse of something sacred happens
                in its glistening descent   some kind   of
                tender eternity

I'll be at the beach – will you join or call me? on a yellow post-it in *her*
                                                               handwriting

I observe   her
As we observe   her
As she observes *her*
And in her I see her and her and her and her and her and her

iv.
Toni Morrison says *beauty is what we were born for*

Wendy and I eat this up like birthday cake
Expand and burst with it
Drown in it

We will never come up for air

Sad boys are not my kink

but in the dream Sad Boy is wearing a suit made entirely of post-it notes that say things like 'We blamed youth and distance' / 'I think I was just scared of having something real' / 'I wish we had tried again' / 'You were so easy to love and you had absolutely no idea' / 'I leave my phone on at night in case you decide you need me' / 'I still leave a space for you in the bed - I wish you were here' / 'I hope you think about me once in a while' and Sad Boy is well hidden beneath them all like a piece of rice under the sofa and he has never looked sexier.

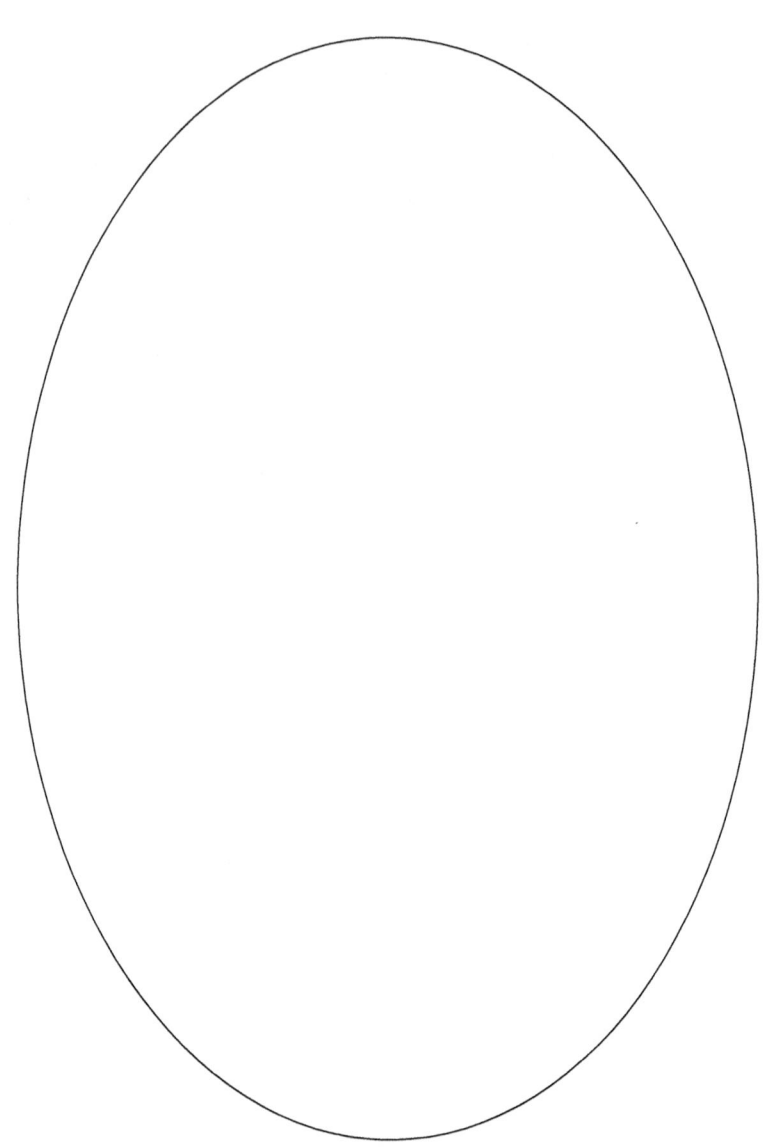

Acknowledgments:

Thank you to the following publications who have previously published some of the poems in this collection: *Strange Region, Prototype 6, The Rialto, Bad Lillies, The Storms, Dear Reader.*

'Evening Class' and 'To Celebrate' were first published in *'i get lost everywhere, you know this now'* by Galia Admoni and Wendy Allen, Salo Press 2024

'Wendy and I both feel ugly at the beauty exhibition' was first published in *'Art Sundays'* by Galia Admoni and Wendy Allen, Salo Press 2025

www.ingramcontent.com/pod-product-compliance
Lightning Source LLC
Chambersburg PA
CBHW060406080526
44583CB00012B/491